People of the Passion

A Lenten Weekly Study

Dr. Cathy Randall

CSS Publishing Company, Inc.
Lima, Ohio

FIRST EDITION
Copyright © 2014
by CSS Publishing Co., Inc.

For more information about CSS Publishing Company resources, visit our website at www. csspub.com, email us at csr@csspub.com, or call (800) 241-4056.

Electronic version of this book:
ISBN-13: 978-0-7880-2770-3
ISBN-10: 978-0-7880-2770-0

ISBN-13: 978-0-7880-2769-7
ISBN-10: 0-7880-2769-7   PRINTED IN USA

Acknowledgments

What do we have that we have not received?
The Rev. Dr. John Rowan Claypool IV

Nothing appears in this volume that I have not received from others. Failing to mention the contributions of some is no indication of a lack of gratitude, just a lack of memory.

I will never, ever forget the generosity of Dr. Brent Landau, currently in the Religious Studies Department of the University of Texas-Austin. As I was preparing this curriculum, I attended Christ Church Cambridge near Harvard Yard while visiting my daughter. God's prevenient grace led my steps there. Dr. Landau was then a Th.D. student at Harvard Divinity School and was teaching a Sunday school class titled "Personalities of the New Testament." The handouts he gave were an absolute goldmine of information. He not only said "feel free to share them with anyone," but later, as I adapted the curriculum to this manuscript, he once again offered, "Feel free to use what I wrote in adapting it to a written manuscript." What a gift! He is without question the co-author of this book.

Rev. Steven Molin of Roseville Lutheran Church, Roseville, Minnesota, was extraordinarily gracious to grant permission for the use of the marvelous exercise from his sermon series for Lent and Easter, *Journey of Stones*. Rev. Charles Durham of First Presbyterian Church, Tuscaloosa, Alabama, had recommended it highly, for which I am eternally grateful.

The sermon given by The Rev. Dr. Samuel T. Lloyd III of Trinity Episcopal Church, Boston, Massachusetts, on Nicodemus in 2002 instantly became a treasured document in our family. It not only described richly the complete transformation of a prominent man, but it was so exquisitely written that I just had to share it virtually intact. How generous of Dr. Lloyd to allow it. His dear friend and mine, Ann Claypool Beard, connected us, as she connects me to the Holy upon every moment with her.

A fourth foundational part of the work is a definition of "blessed" that I once heard attributed to dear Brother Robert Hugh SSF of Little Portion Friary, Mount Sinai, New York. Jill M. Burzynski, administrative assistant at the Friary's Guesthouse, went to great lengths to connect us, and Br. Hugh most kindly allowed me to quote that brilliant insight.

My spiritual director, The Rev. Sandra DePriest of Good Shepherd Episcopal Church in Columbus, Mississippi, used the curriculum as part of her Lenten study and was a tremendous encourager in the process of publishing it. The Rev. David Meginniss, rector of my parish, Christ Episcopal Church in Tuscaloosa, Alabama, took time that I know he does not have to pour over the manuscript for pivotal improvements: from tiny errors to huge contributions from his knowledge of biblical Greek.

CSS Publishing Company was every author's dream publishing house, and Missy Cotrell there an absolute joy with whom to collaborate.

How I wish I could name every single individual who participated in this Lenten study. Their faithfulness to the observance of a Holy Lent and to their church in every season is an inspiration, and their affirmation of the value of this study filled the experience with blessings for me. May it bring blessings into your life as well.

Any list of acknowledgments of gratitude from me would be incomplete without the names of Jaynie Rogers Randall Lilley, Kate Randall Danella, and H. Pettus Randall IV, who bring joy beyond compare to their mother. Their father, H. Pettus Randall III, lives in them on earth and continues to be the source of my deepest gratitude to God. That that great man of God loved me for one day was more than I deserved, and I thank God for giving me almost 32 years of those days.

For God's hand in this work and in all things, I give most humble and hearty thanks.

Cathy Randall
September 2013
Tuscaloosa, Alabama

Table of Contents

Introduction

People of the Passion: A Lenten Weekly Study is a book for churches, prayer groups, or Bible study groups for use to help Christians of all denominations experience more deeply and richly the growth opportunity that is Lent. Each week, a major participant in Jesus' last week of life will be studied: Mary, Mary Magdalene, Peter, Nicodemus, Pilate, and Judas. These individuals represent a continuum of human responses to Jesus: faithfulness, gratitude, conflict, power, and betrayal. We will work to see ourselves in each of them and in each of the human responses to Jesus which they represent.

Instructor's Guide

- Before each class, instructors should place a palm-size piece of jagged stone at each seat and a cross at the exit of the room with enough space for the participants to leave stones at the end of each class. These stones are to be removed by Easter Sunday morning.
- The statement of purpose should be projected on a screen or placed on a poster at the beginning of each class.
- Excerpts from the film *The Passion of the Christ* are suggested as an aid to deepen our understanding.
- Instructors are encouraged to invite a different member of the class to read aloud each of the referenced passages from the Bible or the *Book of Common Prayer*, either from their own Bibles and prayer books, or from copies of the passages distributed in class.
- Although the course is designed for a one-hour class for each of the five weeks of Lent that begin after the week of Ash Wednesday and conclude before Holy Week, Week Four could be divided easily into two sessions if six sessions are desired. Furthermore, if seven sessions are desired, the seventh session could consist of small group discussions where participants share the lessons learned and summary reports are presented to the entire class.
- To the extent that learning is enhanced by repetition, the bracketed words in the following chapters are important especially for those who join the study after the first week.

Faithfulness

Week One
Mary, Mother of Jesus

Let us pray

*O God above us, God before us, God within us, O Father,
Son, and Holy Spirit, be now between us, a bridge across
which your truth can move. In Jesus' name we pray. Amen.*[1]

The purpose of this Lenten weekly study on the People
of the Passion is the purpose of Lent as defined in the *Book
of Common Prayer*:

*To observe with great devotion the days of Jesus' suffer-
ing and resurrection.*
*It is the Church's custom to prepare for this observance
by "a season of penitence and fasting... (because) of the
need which all Christians continually have to renew repentance and faith...*
*(The Church invites us) to the observance of a Holy Lent
by self-examination and repentance; by prayer, fasting, and
self-denial; and by reading and meditating on God's holy
word."*[2]

This series will help us to read and meditate on God's
holy word and to pray together. We shall also engage in self-
denial and fasting by giving up our time and, in some cases,
a meal that we would share. Furthermore, the series will as-
sist us in self-examination as we honestly look for ourselves
in these People of the Passion and therefore repent.

An exercise that we will use each week comes with permission from The Rev. Steven Molin's *Journey of Stones*.[3]
Please hold in your hands the piece of stone before you. No-

11

tice that it is not smooth; the edges are sharp and jagged as if broken. We have a choice this week — and every week of Lent — as to what to do with these stones. We can hang onto them as painful reminders of our separation from God, making us broken people. Or we can let them go; we can lay them at the foot of the Cross and open our hands and hearts so that God can fill them with love and forgiveness, healing, and grace.

As we examine these People of the Passion, let us look for ourselves in them, for those characteristics that we need to lay at the foot of the Cross during this Lent. And perhaps on Easter morning this year, the stone will be moved away for us, just as it was on that first Easter morning.

The Church has placed importance on this penitential season as a way for us to grow to Easter. We are an Easter people, we know the end of the story, but we ignore the grace and opportunity of Lent at our peril. For in Lent, we are called and given an opportunity to remember. Think of the verb "remember" as the opposite of "dismember," of tearing things apart. By remembering, pieces can be put back together. Let us hope that the pieces of our lives "dismembered" in the past can be put back together in the process of our Lenten remembering this year.

This study is not necessarily an intellectual exercise. We are not called to comprehend fully the events of the Passion. As *Forward Day by Day* has said, "Rather than explain what Jesus did on the Cross, we must live it. Somehow, we must find Christ in our own suffering, receive his hope in the midst of our own despair. Somehow, we must find a way to allow him to rescue us out of hell, to reach through the gate of death and haul us mightily into eternal life. This is not primarily an exercise of the understanding, but of the combination of heart and will in which we most clearly sense the Spirit. Heart and will combine to surrender to it, to live into it, and allow it to grow in us."[4]

We are invited to the observance of a Holy Lent where we will remember the Passion, live into it, and allow the growth for which we were created.

The first of the People of the Passion whom we will study is **Mary, Mother of Jesus**. According to Dr. Brent Landau,[5] she is the most famous woman in the world, yet we know only this from the Bible:

* One of the four gospels never even mentions her name, nor does the apostle Paul appear to have any concrete knowledge of her.

* In the gospel of Mark, Mary appears on two (or perhaps three) occasions. In the first instance (3:20-35), Jesus is teaching among a large crowd, and his family comes to restrain him because they think he is "out of his mind." When his mother (Mary's name is not given) and siblings bid him to come outside, Jesus refuses to recognize them, instead recognizing those who do "the will of God" as his family. In 6:3, incredulous bystanders to Jesus' teaching in his hometown of Nazareth ask: "Is not this the carpenter, the son of Mary?" The omission of any mention of Jesus' father suggests that he is no longer living at this time (and later portrayals of Joseph as a carpenter may actually be based on this statement). Finally, there is a "Mary mother of James the younger and Joses" mentioned in 15:40, 47; 16:1 as one of the women who witnesses the crucifixion, burial, and empty tomb. However, many scholars dispute that this refers to Jesus' mother, since it would be odd not to state her relationship to Jesus.

* John's gospel portrays Jesus' mother on two occasions but never names her as Mary. She appears in the very poignant narrative of the wedding at Cana, the site of Jesus' first mir-

acle (2:1-11). She informs him that the wedding has run out of wine, though it is unclear why she is there in the first place. As in Mark, he treats his mother rather rudely: "Woman, what concern is that to you and to me? My hour has not yet come" (2:4). Jesus' mother still tells the servants to obey him, and the changing of water into wine transpires. She also appears at the foot of the Cross in 19:25-27 with Mary Magdalene and a "Mary the wife of Clopas." She is standing next to the "disciple whom he loved," to whom Jesus entrusts her with the words, "Here is your mother" (immediately preceded by "Woman, here is your son"). From that moment on, the gospel says, the disciple took Jesus' mother into his house. Since the Beloved Disciple is often thought to be John, and since John was believed to have traveled to Ephesus after Jesus' death, a tradition began to develop that Mary spent her remaining days in this city of Asia Minor. Incidentally, in 2007 Pope Benedict XVI visited a pilgrimage site outside of Ephesus thought to have been Mary's house.

* Of course, Mary is best known for her presence in the infancy narratives of Matthew and Luke, but these depictions are quite different. In Matthew 1-2, Mary never speaks. She conceives through the Holy Spirit before her marriage to Joseph, but all information about the child is communicated to Joseph through dreams.

* The Mary familiar to us is the one known from Luke's gospel: Jesus' conception is announced to her through a visitation from the angel Gabriel (1:26-38); she sings the beautiful hymn known as the *Magnificat* (1:46-55); she travels with Joseph from Nazareth to Bethlehem because of the census and lays her firstborn in a manger (2:5-7). Other details unique to Luke's infancy narrative are Mary's treasuring in her heart of the shepherd's story, the elder Simeon's cryptic prophecy to Mary that "a sword will pierce your own soul,"

and the events in Jerusalem when Jesus is twelve (2:19, 35, 41-51).

So this is Mary's story, putting in chronological order what we know from the Bible: Mary is first introduced in scripture as a young virgin engaged to Joseph, a descendant of Abraham and David. According to Jewish custom, an engagement was linked to marriage in such a way that the fiancée was called "wife." According to Jewish law, if a wife were unfaithful during the engagement, just as during marriage, she would be stoned to death.

During her engagement, Mary was visited at her home in Nazareth by the angel Gabriel, who said to her, "Greetings, favored one! The Lord is with you" (Luke 1:28). Mary was evidently frightened at the angel's visit, since Gabriel told her not to be afraid. He then announced that she would become pregnant and have a child who would be called the Son of the Most High; he would inherit the throne of King David and reign forever. Mary answered, "How can this be, since I am a virgin?" (Luke 1:34). She did not doubt what Gabriel said but was confused about how it could happen. The angel explained that Mary would become pregnant by the power of the Holy Spirit, and she accepted this assignment for her life in spite of the shame and danger she would experience because of her pregnancy.

Mary received some other good news from Gabriel: Her older relative Elizabeth had conceived a son six months earlier and was going to have a baby after a long life of childlessness. In Mary's joy, she traveled to the city of Judah in the hill country (about eighty miles from Nazareth) to visit Elizabeth and her husband Zechariah. When Mary arrived at their house and greeted them, the baby in Elizabeth's womb (John the Baptist) leaped for joy to hear the voice of the mother of Jesus. Elizabeth exuberantly expressed in a loud voice:

Blessed are you among women, and blessed is the child you will bear! But why am I so favored, that the mother of my Lord should come to me? As soon as the sound of your greeting reached my ears, the baby in my womb leaped for joy. Blessed is she who has believed that what the Lord has said to her will be accomplished! (Luke 1:42-45)

An apocryphal text from the first half of the second century, known as the Infancy Gospel (or Protevangelium) of James, fills in many of the details of Mary's life up to Jesus' birth. This gospel is not a part of the canon and therefore is not considered authoritative, but believers can choose whether the background information it provides is helpful to an understanding of Mary.

According to the text, she is born to an infertile couple, Joachim and Anna, after Anna is visited by an angel. They promise that the child shall only serve the Lord, and at age three Mary goes to live in the Jerusalem Temple. When she turns twelve, the priests of the temple decide she must leave so as not to pollute the temple. They gather together all the widowers from Israel, and through a miraculous sign, the widower Joseph is chosen to be Mary's husband. In this text he is an old man and has grown children, making sense of Jesus' "brothers and sisters" in the gospels and fostering the developing traditions of Mary's perpetual virginity. With the exception of several other interesting details, the rest of the text largely follows the infancy narratives of Matthew and Luke.

Lesley Hazleton says that each of these new images takes us away from the real Mary. What we know from the Bible is that Mary stayed close to Jesus.[6] She accompanied him throughout his ministry, and she accompanied him to his Cross. Let us use the nearness/separation continuum as a theme threading through the six individuals whom we study this Lent. The word "sin" is connected to "separation," "estrangement," "outside." The ancient Greek word *h'amartia* is a word translated in English as "sin." It derives from an archery term meaning "to shoot with the aim to miss" or to "miss the target." Mary did not stay outside the presence of the Lord; she did not separate herself from Jesus, even when he rebuked her. She stayed close even when it would have been easier to separate. She embraced the pain that closeness involved. She grieved — fully — on Good Friday and even before, as the reality of her son's destiny became increasingly clear. And by staying close, she witnessed Easter; she became an Easter person. Those who separated did not.

On the weekend after my 57-year-old husband Pettus was diagnosed with terminal pancreatic cancer, a caption from a church publication leapt off the page at me: "By being good, we are allowed to live the most deeply satisfying of lives as it is the life closest to the life of God, not a life you understand without pain, but a life filled with joy."[7] It appeared almost as a dare: Let's see if you can know a life filled with joy now, you who have been sheltered and spoiled all your life. A life filled with joy has been easy. In the face of losing the heart of your heart, can you embrace that pain and still have a life filled with joy? Can you stay close to the life of God, embrace the life that is before you, now that it is filled with such pain?

Staying close to Jesus and embracing the abundance of life that we are given, not separating ourselves from it, is Mary's answer. The importance of such presence is captured in the following story:

A nurse took the tired, anxious serviceman to the bedside. "Your son is here," she whispered to the patient in the bed. She had to repeat the words several times before the patient's eyes opened. Heavily sedated because of the pain of his heart attack, he dimly saw the young uniformed Marine standing outside the oxygen tent. He reached out his

17

hand. The Marine wrapped his toughened fingers around the old man's limp ones, squeezing a message of love and encouragement. The nurse brought a chair so that the Marine could sit beside the bed. He sat there all night long in the poorly lighted ward, holding the old man's hand and offering him words of love and strength. Occasionally, the nurse suggested that the Marine move away and rest a while. Whenever the nurse entered the ward, the Marine was oblivious of her and of the night noises of the hospital. Now and then, she heard him say a few gentle words. The dying man said nothing, only held tightly to his son all through the night.

Toward dawn, the old man passed away. The Marine went to tell the nurse. While she did what she had to do, he waited. Finally, the nurse returned. She started to offer words of sympathy, but the Marine interrupted her. "Who was that man?" he asked. The nurse was startled, "He was your father," she answered. "No, he wasn't," the Marine replied. "I never saw him before in my life." "Then why didn't you say something when I took you to him?" "Well," the Marine said, "I knew right away there'd been a mistake. But I also knew that he needed his son, and his son just wasn't here. When I realized that he was too sick to tell whether or not I was his son, knowing how much he needed me, I stayed close."

That's what we're called to do: to be present, to stay close, and to stay close to our Lord and Savior Jesus Christ by staying close to neighbors. The story ends in this way: We are not human beings going through a temporary spiritual experience. We are spiritual beings going through a temporary human experience.

My son Pettus had an almost identical experience when working in Mother Teresa's Home for the Dying. He noticed a man gasping for breath, and when he raced to the sisters to help the patient, they said that the man was dying and that there was nothing that they could do to save him. So Pettus asked permission to hold his hand until he took his last breath. By staying close, he gained experience and insight that empowered him to stay close at the moment that his beloved father entered the fullness of life and joy. At the end, the only thing Mary could do for her Son was to be close to him, but far more than his need of her, Mary needed to be present to Jesus so that he could make all things new in her. She did not shake her fist at God in anger or clutch her arms around herself in the paralysis of grief. She opened her arms, she raced to her Son, and she stayed as close to him as she could. From the moment when she said "yes" to the angel Gabriel, she embraced both the joy and the pain of loving with its inevitability of losing — and she experienced Easter.

If the instructor is using the movie *The Passion of the Christ*, please watch a scene that portrays Mary's embrace of both the joy and pain of loving with its inevitability of losing, found at the following point in the film: 1:14:45–1:19:00. Please notice how young Mary is (probably mid- to late-40s) and that the woman chosen to play Mary is a Romanian from a Jewish family, therefore with different characteristics from so many of the Western European depictions with which we have become familiar.

In conclusion tonight, after watching the clip, please ask yourself the following questions.

---

1. Prayer of The Rev. Dr. John Rowan Claypool IV.

2. *Book of Common Prayer*, p. 264.

3. The Rev. Steven Molin, *Journey of Stones* (Lima, Ohio: CSS Publishing Company, 2002), p. 15.

4. Anonymous, *Forward Day by Day* (Cincinnati, Ohio: Forward Movement, February 21, 2007).

5. Brent Landau, "Personalities of the New Testament," Sunday school class handout at Christ Church, Cambridge, Massachusetts, 2006, used with permission.

6. Lesley Hazelton, *Mary: A Flesh-and-Blood Biography of the Virgin Mother* (New York: Bloomsbury, 2005).

7. The Rt. Rev. Marc Andrus, *The Apostle* (Birmingham, Alabama: Episcopal Diocese of Alabama, February 2002).

QUESTIONS
(for small group discussion or journaling)

What about yourself did you see in Mary?

What do you wish you had seen?

What do you wish you had NOT seen and need to let go?

When the film ends, let us depart from this place in silence, and if you wish, lay the stone of your grief at the foot of the Cross before leaving the room.

Gratitude

Week Two
Mary Magdalene

Let us pray

*O God above us, God before us, God within us, O Father,
Son, and Holy Spirit, be now between us, a bridge across
which your truth can move. In Jesus' name we pray. Amen.*

[Let us be reminded from Week One of the purpose of this
Lenten weekly study on the People of the Passion. It is the
very purpose of Lent as defined in the *Book of Common
Prayer*:

> *To observe with great devotion the days of Jesus' suffer-
> ing and resurrection.*
> *It is the Church's custom to prepare for this observance
> by "a season of penitence and fasting... (because) of the
> need which all Christians continually have to renew repen-
> tance and faith...*
> *(The Church invites us) to the observance of a Holy Lent
> by self-examination and repentance; by prayer, fasting, and
> self-denial; and by reading and meditating on God's holy
> word."*[1]

You may hold in your hands pieces of stone and notice
that they are not smooth; the edges are sharp and jagged as
if broken. We have a choice this week — and every week
of Lent — as to what to do with those stones. We can hang
onto them as painful reminders of our separation from God,
making us broken people. Or we can let them go; we can lay
them at the foot of the Cross and open our hands and hearts
so that God can fill them with love and forgiveness, healing,

and grace.

So as we examine these People of the Passion, let us look for us in them, for those characteristics that we need to lay at the foot of the Cross during this Lent. And perhaps on this Easter morning, the stone will be moved away for us, just as it was on that first Easter morning.]

Last week, we looked for ourselves in Mary, the mother of Jesus. We discussed how little the Bible tells us about the most famous woman in the world. It only took nine minutes to tell the story that we can piece together chronologically from the scriptural references. Some of the parts of myself that I saw in her included grief, disappointment when life didn't turn out the way she'd expected, confusion as life's whirlwind hit her, so many things in me that I need to let go. But her absolute steadfastness in staying close to Jesus regardless of her fear and pain is something I need to take on. She accompanied him throughout his ministry, and she accompanied him to his Cross. Let's continue to use the nearness/separation continuum as a theme threading through our study of these six individuals.

[The word "sin" is connected to "separation," "estrangement," "outside." Mary did not stay outside the presence of the Lord; she did not separate herself from Jesus, even when he rebuked her. She stayed close even when it would have been easier to separate. She embraced the pain that closeness involved. She grieved — fully — on Good Friday and even before as the reality of her son's destiny became increasingly clear. And by staying close, she witnessed Easter; she became an Easter person. Those who separated did not.]

Mary Magdalene is another who stayed close. According to Brent Landau,[2]

WHAT MARY MAGDALENE WAS NOT:

* Was Mary Magdalene the woman taken in adultery (John 8:1-11)? This is "a late addition to John's text, not a part of the original gospel. Scribes were so uncertain where it belonged that some, according to Bruce Chilton, added it at different places in John... or to Luke"![3]

* Was Mary Magdalene Jesus' lover/wife/mother of his child? The New Testament gives no indication that Jesus was married, and even if it was uncommon for a Jewish man of his time to remain single, it was not unheard of (both John the Baptist and Paul seem to have been unmarried). Nor do the canonical gospels say anything that suggests a romantic relationship between Jesus and Mary. The only ancient ostensibly Christian writing that hints at such a situation is the third-century gospel of Philip, which says that Jesus "loved her more than all the disciples, and he used to kiss her on her..." [the text breaks off here, unfortunately]. This gospel is not a part of the canon and therefore is not considered authoritative, but believers can choose whether the background information it provides is helpful to an understanding of Mary Magdalene. The idea that Jesus had a child with Mary Magdalene (as *The DaVinci Code* claims) does not appear in any ancient text and is a much more recent hypothesis. However, traditions in the Middle Ages exist stating that Mary lived out the rest of her days in France.

* Was Mary Magdalene a prostitute? The gospels say nothing to indicate that this was the case. Starting with Pope Gregory the Great in the sixth century, Mary Magdalene begins to be linked with the unnamed "woman in the city, who was a sinner" in Luke 7:36-50 who anoints and kisses Jesus' feet. But Mary is introduced in Luke's gospel two verses later (Luke

8:2), and there is nothing to suggest that she had already made an appearance.

* According to Bruce Chilton,[4] a prostitute would not have been allowed into the Pharisee's home. But the woman there, like all of us, was a sinful person to some extent, whether she was a prostitute or not. Instead of prostitution, Chilton suggests perhaps her sinfulness was a series of husbands, she married outside her class, or she was a hairdresser, an occupation considered sinful in those days.

Chilton believes that Mary Magdalene might have been the sinful woman of the city. Read without this inference, Mark breaks Jesus' promise that "wherever the good news is proclaimed in the whole world, what she has done will be told in remembrance of her" (Mark 14:9).

* *The DaVinci Code* suggests in its fictional story that the Holy Grail, Jesus' chalice at the Last Supper, was actually Mary Magdalene. As these words from the discussions reverberated: "open hands and hearts so God can fill," "surrender," "allow growth," "say yes," "emptying (fasting)," I was reminded of an image of the chalice and of the first prayer in which I was ever led by The Rev. Dr. John Claypool. Please observe first, and then join me in this silent prayer.

Bending over from a standing position, we extend our arms to the ground and scoop up all of the hurts and problems and failures of our lives. As we rise to a standing position, we bring our arms to our heart and then lift our arms to release everything to heaven. With our arms now forming the bowl of a chalice, we receive the grace of God poured to the full, and then bring that grace to our hearts. Finally, we bend over and again extend our arms to the ground, pouring out the grace of God to the earth and to all of our brothers and sisters.

Please stand and join me in this silent prayer.

If the instructor is using the movie, let's watch Mary Magdalene's first encounter with Jesus as depicted in the film *The Passion of the Christ*, located at 1:06:11–1:07:45. Whatever her sin, whether or not she was the woman taken in adultery or the sinful woman of the city, I can see Mary Magdalene crawling to Jesus' feet after having been saved by him from whatever her sin was. As I see her face, I am reminded of the words "lost in wonder, love, and praise" from the hymn "Love Divine, All Loves Excelling."

According to Dr. Landau[5]:
WHAT THE BIBLE SAYS MARY MAGALENE WAS:

* One of the most prominent female followers of Jesus, although no gospel explains how she came to know him.

* Mary Magdalene seems to have come from a city on the Sea of Galilee by the name of Magdala or Tarichaeae. The city is never mentioned in the Bible apart from Mary Magdalene, but the Jewish historian Josephus says it had about 40,000 inhabitants and was predominantly Gentile. Later rabbinic tradition states that it fell to the Romans in the Jewish War because of its poor moral character.

* Luke 8:2 says that Mary was one of several women who followed Jesus around Galilee and provided for his group out of their own means. Chilton identifies Joanna as wealthy but states that Mary Magdalene was not necessarily wealthy. This passage (along with Mark 16:9, a later addition to Mark's gospel) states that seven demons had come forth from Mary. This presumably means that Jesus had performed an exorcism upon her, but the gospels give no further explanation of these demons. His Spirit drove out the unclean spirits in her

and installed his in the vacuum. The kingdom of God arrived in her, and her gratitude drove her to stay close to him for the rest of his life.

* She plays a crucial role in the Passion narrative as a witness to Jesus' death (Mark 15:40), burial (Mark 15:47), the empty tomb (Mark 16:1), and the resurrection (John 20:11-18). She often appears in these scenes with a small group of other women, which is not surprising since many traditional cultures give women the responsibility for mourning and caring for the dead.

* The scene of John 20:11-18 is the most dramatic of these accounts. After finding the tomb empty and informing the disciples, Mary Magdalene returns to the tomb and weeps. She first sees two angels standing at the place where he was buried, and turning around, she sees Jesus without recognizing him. She thinks he is the gardener and asks him to tell her where Jesus' body has been taken. Mary finally realizes it is Jesus when he calls her by name, and then he curiously tells her not to touch him (compare Matthew 28:9-10, where the women hold on to Jesus' feet).

* In several passages (Mark 16:9-11; Luke 24:10-11; John 20:18), Mary acts as the "apostle to the apostles," going and telling Jesus' disciples the good news of the resurrection, but in two of these accounts, the disciples do not believe her. Despite these attestations as the first witness to the resurrection, Mary does not appear in the list of those to whom the resurrected Jesus appears in Paul's first letter to the Corinthians (1 Corinthians 15:5-6).

* An apocryphal gospel (remember the above warnings about such writings) exists that is attributed to Mary Magdalene, although it likely dates from the second century and

is not directly traceable to her. She acts as a consoler for the distraught apostles after Jesus' death, and she also has a visionary experience where Jesus communicates teachings to her. Andrew and Peter ridicule her vision, but a disciple named Levi defends her as the Lord's favorite.

If she is not the woman taken in adultery, not the wife/ lover of Jesus, and not even the woman who anoints him at the Pharisee's home, then what is the most important thing we know about her?

Mary Magdalene's experience at the tomb is the key to the gospel as written. The most important message in the gospels is that Jesus rose from the dead, and he conquered sin and death for all of us. And Mary Magdalene GOT IT. In every other resurrection account in the gospels, the others who encounter Jesus express confusion about his identity or the truth of his resurrected existence. Only the women, on the basis of what they directly perceived, knew the significance of what they saw, and they knew it immediately. Could that have been because they stayed close to him and the others did not?

As Mark uses *theoreo* for "see" rather than *horao* (the verb for physical seeing), the women's visionary discernment literally becomes a matter of deep perception rather than ordinary vision. They GOT IT. When the angelic young man told them in Mark 16:6-7, "Do not be alarmed; you are looking for Jesus of Nazareth, who was crucified. He has been raised; he is not here. Look, there is the place they laid him. But go, tell his disciples and Peter that he is going ahead of you to Galilee; there you will see him, just as he told you," they GOT IT. When the others saw Jesus later, they did not immediately GET IT: the two disciples on the walk to Emmaus (Luke 24:13-32), Thomas (John 20:24-29), and on the beach (John 21:1-14). Mary Magadalene *perceived* immediately when she *saw*. Was that because she, unlike the others, stayed close? The others separated, hid, stayed outside: some of the synonyms of "sin."

Perhaps the most important thing we can learn from Mary Magdalene is that, if we want to GET IT, we, like she, need to stay close. At the moment Jesus cast out her seven demons, she said "yes." She stayed with him from that moment until he died. He was the focus of her life, and she continued to serve him after his death and all her days.

----

1. *Book of Common Prayer*, p. 264.

2. Brent Landau, *op cit.*

3. Bruce Chilton, *Mary Magdalene: A Biography* (New York: Doubleday, 2005).

4. *Ibid.*

5. Brent Landau, *op cit.*

QUESTIONS
(for small group discussion or journaling)

What about yourself did you see in Mary Magdalene?

What do you wish you had seen?

What do you wish you had NOT seen and need to let go?

This stone represents for me the demons that distract me from focusing on him, from staying close to him, from perceiving him. I invite you to join me in silence as we leave to let go of this stone at the foot of the Cross before leaving the room, in the sure and certain hope that on Easter morning, this stone will be rolled away as it was on the first Easter morning.

Conflict

Week Three
Peter

Let us pray

O God above us, God before us, God within us, O Father, Son, and Holy Spirit, be now between us, a bridge across which your truth can move. In Jesus' name we pray. Amen.

Half of our Lenten journey will be completed with this lesson. Congratulations on your self-discipline, self-denial, prayer, and meditation as you fulfill the purpose of Lent. One suggested devotional says:

I have never known God to withhold the truth from people with the will to strive for it. And I have never known the struggle to be easy... God does not bring us together in order that we should not grow in wisdom and moral stature. God doesn't bring the church together in order that the joy of life in harmony with God's gracious will should elude us. That's what the church is for: to sustain the people of God in their journey together toward union (closeness) with God. God is not interested in our going backward or remaining where we are. We want a closer walk with God, not a more distant one. And that is what God wants too.[1]

A theme that continues to thread through the study of these People of the Passion, these individuals who were witnesses of Christ's Passion, is the continuum of nearness vs. separation. As we have discussed, the word "sin" is derived from the word for "separation" or "outside." It is also derived from *adikaius*, which means "out of right relationship." On the other hand, Brother Robert Hugh, a Franciscan friar, has been quoted as saying that "nearness to God" also can be defined by the word "blessed." The extent to which these individuals stayed close to Christ is the extent to which they were blessed and became Easter people. Mary, mother of Jesus, and Mary Magdalene stayed close, and they saw the resurrection. Jesus' mother did not let his rebuffs or her own bewilderment or fear separate her from him. She fought through crowds to stay as close as she could. Mary Magdalene was so overwhelmed with gratitude that he had healed her of seven demons, of mental illness that had robbed her of focus on life, of participation in life, that she followed him the rest of his life. Like Mary, the mother of Jesus, Mary Magdalene said "yes" to Jesus; she stayed close to Jesus, and therefore she was the first one who GOT IT, who perceived the most important message of the gospel: Jesus rose from the dead.

One of the ways we can stay close to Jesus is through regular Bible reading. The following devotional is instructive:

A lifetime of reading Holy Scriptures is very much like a long marriage: the two of you sit down to breakfast across from each other for thirty or forty years, and you think you know each other completely, and then one of you says something so surprising, so unexpected, and you realize you haven't scratched the surface of this human being to whom you are closer than you are to anyone else in the world. [Studying] the Bible is just like that: you get to thinking you know what's in there, but then one day you open the book and there is something you've just never seen before. And suddenly a piece of the Bible has a whole new significance it did not have before. And you may have read that passage a thousand times. Sometimes it is time for a moment of insight. They just don't come until their time arrives, so we'd better be on the alert for them. You can see something for decades without

really seeing its importance in your life, and then one day
you look at it and suddenly there it is.[2]

The story of Peter is so familiar to all of us. I pray that
this week, as we remember Peter, we will look for ourselves
in him, and in so doing RE-MEMBER ourselves, put ourselves back together in a more complete, more perfect way.

Before we begin to study Peter, let us be reminded of
our purpose here: The purpose of this Lenten weekly study
of the People of the Passion is the very purpose of Lent as
defined in the *Book of Common Prayer*:

To observe with great devotion the days of Jesus' suffer-
ing and resurrection.

It is the Church's custom to prepare for this observance
by "a season of penitence and fasting... (because) of the
need which all Christians continually have to renew repen-
tance and faith...

(The Church invites us) to the observance of a Holy Lent
by self-examination and repentance; by prayer, fasting, and
self-denial; and by reading and meditating on God's holy
word."[3]

As we go through our "self-examination," I invite you
once again to hold in your hand a piece of stone. Notice that
it is not smooth; the edges are sharp and jagged as if broken.
We have a choice this week — and every week of Lent — as
to what to do with those stones. We can hang onto them as
painful reminders of our separation from God, making us
broken people. Or we can let them go; we can lay them at the
foot of the Cross and open our hands and hearts so that God
can fill them with love and forgiveness, healing, and grace.

So as we examine these People of the Passion, let's look
for us in them, for those characteristics that we need to lay
at the foot of the Cross during this Lent. And perhaps on this

Easter morning the stone will be moved away for us just as it was on that first Easter morning.

If the instructor is using the movie, let us watch the lowest point in Peter's life as we watch the excerpt from the film *The Passion of the Christ* located at 29:14–31:40.

We can see the effects of staying close to Jesus vs. separating from him in this one human being, perhaps even more dramatically than comparing among all of those whom we study this Lent.

NEAR ———————————————————————————— FAR
Mary Mary Magdalene PETER Pilate Nicodemus   Judas

What a great description of Peter's life is the title of Pope John Paul II's *Crossing the Threshold of Hope*. Peter did cross the threshold of hope; under the influence of hope and faith and love, he moved closer to Jesus. But like most of us, he slid back outside. When his focus turned to self instead of to his Lord, he separated. And he did so again and again and again, like most of us. But Peter always returned. The pattern of his life was much like the story they tell of the little boy who always wondered what the monks did in the monastery on the hill above the village. When he saw one of the monks in the marketplace, he asked him, "Sir, what do you monks do all day up there?" The monk replied, "Son, we fall down and we get up. We fall down and we get up. We fall down and we get up." As we study Peter tonight, let's hear his story chronologically according to the biblical sources and watch for those moments where he crossed the threshold of hope, coming closer to his Lord.

The story of the drunk who gets into a fight in a bar has a moral that is reminiscent of Peter. When the police come to break up the fight, they read the drunk his rights: "You have the right to remain silent...." "Well," the drunk says, as

he tells the story later, "I had the RIGHT to remain silent…
I just didn't have the ABILITY." He does not remain silent,
having a verbal altercation with the police, and he is thrown
in jail.[4]

At each of the crucial moments in Peter's life, he has
the God-given right to stay close, to follow the will of God,
but in many of them, being intoxicated by his own will, he
does not have the ability. The ability came later, when he
was overpowered by the truth of the hope of the resurrection.
That gave him the ability to preach the gospel to the ends of
his world and to go to a martyr's death.

According to Brent Landau, Peter first lived in Bethsaida
but later resided in Capernaum where he worked as a fisher-
man and where his brother Andrew personally introduced
him to Jesus. Andrew eagerly told Peter that he had found
the Messiah. Upon meeting Peter, Jesus called him by name
(Simon) and then changed his name to Peter (John 1:35-42).
Jesus got in a boat with Peter one day after a fruitless night
of fishing, and Jesus told him to try again (Luke 5:4b-11).

Peter followed. It was not, never has been, and never will
be the will of Jesus or of his Father that we should be separated from God. Nothing "will be able to separate us from
the love of God in Christ Jesus" (Romans 8:39). This is the
first time that Peter crossed the threshold of hope, following close to Jesus. By staying close, he witnessed his own
mother-in-law healed by Jesus (Mark 1:29-31) and was one
of only three to be invited by Jesus to witness his healing
of the daughter of the ruler of the synagogue, Jairus (Mark
5:36b-43). In Matthew 14:25-31, Jesus walks on water near
the disciples' boat during a storm. Jesus tells Peter to come
to him, but after beginning to walk on the water, Peter becomes afraid and starts to sink, only to be rescued by Jesus.

Witnessing Jesus' mighty works, Peter stays close. Because of that, when Jesus asks "Who do you say that I am?"
Peter is the first to give the correct answer, to make sense of

what he saw, to perceive what he physically saw: "You are the Christ." But in his very next words, by putting his will above his Lord's, Peter missed the point again (Mark 8:29-33). Peter's missing the point, as all of us do most of the time, is much like the young man who was driving along a winding road on the California coast in his new convertible. Suddenly he saw another convertible coming toward him around the next curve. The driver was a gorgeous woman, so the young man sat up cockily, draping his right wrist over the steering wheel with his left elbow propped on the open door, assuming his "coolest" pose. As her car aligned with his, he looked over to catch her eye as she passed, only to hear her shout, "Pig!" He was deflated. As he rounded the curve from which she had just emerged, he ran into a pig in the middle of the road. He had heard the message but had missed the point. Peter's pre-resurrection life was much like this, often missing the point of Jesus' teaching.

Peter was one of only three invited to witness Jesus' transfiguration (Mark 9:2-8). There, in his exuberance, Peter wanted to build dwellings for the three to keep them close permanently. At the Last Supper, Jesus began to wash the disciples' feet, but Peter recoiled, separating himself from Jesus and refusing to be washed (John 13:4-9). When Jesus said that Peter could have no part of him without the washing, Peter moved close and begged Jesus not just to wash his feet but his hands and his head also. After supper, Jesus predicted that the disciples would abandon him (Mark 14:27-31). And as he promised, Peter showed great bravery when Judas brought the temple guards to arrest Jesus (John 18:10-11). But as Jesus had prophesied, Peter later denied him three times (Luke 22:54-62). After Jesus' prediction of Peter's three denials, Peter had received another invitation to be especially close to Jesus, issued to only three of the disciples. Jesus asked Peter with James and John to wait and watch with him as he prayed in the Garden of Gethsemane

(Mark 14:32-41a).

But Peter was nowhere to be found at the crucifixion, hiding in fear. And there are no gospel accounts of Peter's witnessing the resurrection, only the mention in Luke 24:34 that the men who had walked with Jesus on the Road to Emmaus raced back to the eleven disciples in Jerusalem and told them, *including Peter*, "The Lord has risen indeed and has appeared to Simon."

Peter was part of the groups that saw their risen Lord on numerous occasions, and the power of that vision transformed him once and for all. There is never an account again where, once he crossed the threshold in the hope of the resurrection, he ever slid back. For example, after the resurrection Peter was fishing at night with some of the other disciples, and "just after daybreak, Jesus stood on the beach; but the disciples did not know that it was Jesus...." Jesus said to them, "Come and have breakfast." None of the disciples dared ask him, "Who are you?" because they knew it was the Lord. Jesus came and took the bread and gave it to them, and did the same with the fish. This was now the third time that Jesus appeared to the disciples after he was raised from the dead (John 21:4, 12-15). When they had finished breakfast, Jesus asked Peter three times "Do you love me?" and each time that Peter said "Yes," Jesus said, "Feed my sheep" (John 21:16-17). Jesus told Peter three times what it meant to follow him, one for each of the times that Peter had denied him. From that moment, Peter stayed close to Jesus until the end of his days, although Jesus was as physically absent from Peter as he is from us.

PETER'S ACTIVITIES AFTER THE ASCENSION:

* Paul's letters (often considered the earliest documents of the New Testament) detail several of his meetings with Peter in Jerusalem. After his conversion, Paul went to Peter

possibly to learn about Jesus (Galatians 1:18). Later, Paul accuses Peter of hypocrisy because he initially ate together with Gentiles but then stopped when other leaders of the Jerusalem church criticized him for it (Galatians 2:11-14).

* In the book of Acts, Peter is a prominent member of the Jerusalem community, where he preaches sermons (2:14-36), works as a missionary (8:14-25), and performs miracles (3:1-10). When King Herod Agrippa I begins persecuting members of the Jerusalem church, Peter is put in prison, where he is released later through the help of an angel (12:3-11). After he appears briefly to members of the church, he leaves "for another place" (12:17).

* Was this "other place" Rome? The New Testament does not offer many clues. First Peter 5:13 (an epistle that most scholars believe was not actually written by Peter) sends greetings from the "sister church in Babylon." "Babylon" may be a code-name for Rome, since it also appears on several occasions in the book of Revelation (14:9, 18:21) and probably means Rome. Outside of the New Testament, Peter's residence in Rome is mentioned by a number of early Christian writers (Tertullian and Irenaeus).

Did Peter die as a martyr in Rome? In the New Testament, only John 21:18 mentions Peter's death and does so in cryptic fashion ("when you grow old, you will stretch out your hands, and someone else will fasten a belt around you and take you to where you do not wish to go"). Among early Christian writings, the Acts of Peter (late second/early third century) is the first to record that Peter was crucified upside down. Roman historians state that many Christians in Rome were killed by Nero in 64 AD in the aftermath of a great fire, and some speculate that Peter (and Paul) died then. In 1950 Pope Pius XII announced that Peter's tomb had been discovered below the Vatican, and in 1968 Pope Paul VI announced that the bones of Peter indeed had been found. But controversy surrounds these claims, and few visitors are allowed to see the Roman cemetery under St. Peter's Basilica.

Surely, we think, we could be so transformed if we could see with our eyes the resurrected Jesus. Some, like Thomas and like me, might require more: actually to be invited by Jesus to touch the wounds in his hands and side. The following devotional speaks powerfully to that:

Being able physically to see or hear God wouldn't actually help all that much... a person's spirit is largely hidden from others. We do not know one another well except after long acquaintance and shared history. The disciples, who ate and talked and walked with Jesus every day, were forever getting it wrong about who he was, but they all ended up thinking he was the Messiah eventually. It wasn't something they learned, the way you learn multiplication tables. It was something into which they allowed themselves to grow.

How can you believe, if you don't know anything about God? For we know so very little about God.

We can do what we can. We learn what we can. You explore the spirit of God the same way you explore the spirit of another person: You spend time in God's presence [staying close to him]. You examine your own heart and mind with respect to God. You watch the world for signs of the Spirit. You read what people in the past have felt and thought about it, and talk to people in the present who are also seeking. You sit quietly in meditation and see what comes up.[5]

That sums up what we are doing this very Lent. We are exploring the spirit of God. We are examining our hearts and minds as we examine what about these People of the Passion is like us by studying what people in the past have felt and thought about him. We are talking to each other in the

41

present, with those who also are seeking. We are allowing ourselves to grow by coming as close to Jesus as we can.

---

1. The Rt. Rev. Edmond Browning, *A Year of Days with the Book of Common Prayer* (New York: Ballatine Publishing Group, 1991, March 6).

2. Browning, March 8.

3. *Book of Common Prayer*, p. 264.

4. en.wikiquote.org/wiki/Ron_White

5. Browning, March 11.

QUESTIONS
(for small group discussion or journaling)

What about yourself did you see in Peter?

What do you wish you had seen?

What do you wish you had NOT seen and need to let go?

This study helps me to stay close, helps me to see in Peter that I just do not have the ability to choose nearness over separation most of the time. But thanks be to God, God is choosing nearness to me. Jesus' first words were "Turn around, the kingdom of heaven is at hand." Let's open our hands, by putting at the foot of the Cross the stones that we clinch so tightly, and let him take our open hands in his. One of the many ways we are called to approach God as a child is the following: When you are crossing a busy street with a child, if the child holds onto your hand, you can't really keep the child from danger because the little one can let go whenever s/he chooses. But if the child reaches up to put his or her hand in yours, so that you can exert your will that s/he not perish, the child is safe. May we open our clinched hands, let go of whatever we are holding, and coming close to our heavenly Father, reach up (like the woman taken in adultery in the scene last week) so that he can take our hand in his and lead us through this week, through this Lent, through this life. Please let him lead you in silence now so that you can unclench your hand and leave the stone at his Cross.

Power

Week Four
Pontius Pilate and Nicodemus

Let us pray

Almighty and eternal God, so draw our hearts to you, so guide our minds, so fill our imaginations, so control our wills, that we may be wholly yours, utterly dedicated to you; and then use us, we pray, as you will, and always to your glory and the welfare of your people; through our Lord and Savior Jesus Christ. Amen.[1]

Our recurring motif as we study the People of the Passion is the continuum of nearness vs. separation. As we have discussed, the word "sin" is derived from the word for "separation" or "outside." The word "blessed" could be defined as "nearness to God." And the extent to which these individuals stayed close to Christ is the extent to which they were blessed and became Easter people. Mary, mother of Jesus, and Mary Magdalene stayed close, and they saw the resurrection. Peter crossed and recrossed and recrossed the threshold of hope from separation to nearness, just as we do, but once he perceived the hope of the resurrection, he got it too and spent the rest of his life staying near to his risen Lord.

[Before we begin to study the next individuals, let us be reminded of our purpose here: the purpose of this Lenten weekly study on the People of the Passion is the very purpose of Lent as defined in the *Book of Common Prayer*:

To observe with great devotion the days of Jesus' suffering and resurrection.

It is the Church's custom to prepare for this observance by "a season of penitence and fasting... (because) of the need which all Christians continually have to renew repentance and faith...

(The Church invites us) to the observance of a Holy Lent by self-examination and repentance; by prayer, fasting, and self-denial; and by reading and meditating on God's holy word."[2]

As we go through that "self-examination," I invite you once again to hold in your hand a piece of stone. Its edges are sharp and jagged as if broken. We have a choice this week — and every week of Lent — as to what to do with those stones. We can hang onto them as painful reminders of our separation from God, making us broken people. Or we can let them go; we can lay them at the foot of the Cross and open our hands and hearts so that we can move closer to God and God can fill us with love and forgiveness and healing and grace.

So as we examine these People of the Passion, let us look for ourselves in them, for those characteristics that we need to lay at the foot of the Cross during this Lent. And perhaps on this Easter morning the stone will be moved away for us, just as it was on that first Easter morning.]

We can see the effects of staying close to Jesus vs. separating from him as we look at the six People of the Passion we are studying this Lent.

NEAR ————————————————————————— FAR
Mary Mary Magdalene Peter Pilate Nicodemus   Judas

Let us look at Pontius Pilate. According to Brent Landau, the Bible says little about this man whose name we say every time we recite the Creed.

* Pontius Pilate was a Roman prefect who governed Judea from 26-36 CE. His historical existence is not in doubt, given the mentions of him by two Jewish historians, Philo and Josephus. In 1961 a dedication inscription was found in Caesarea Maritima bearing his name, the only undisputed archaeological evidence for any individual directly associated with Jesus.

* Descriptions of Pilate in Philo and Josephus are almost universally negative and portray him as a very brutal ruler, blatantly disrespectful of Jewish religious sensibilities. Three events here will suffice: 1) Pilate brought into Jerusalem images of the emperor under the cover of night, and only a massive display of nonviolent resistance forced their removal; 2) Pilate built an aqueduct for Jerusalem but took funds from the temple in order to finance it. In the protests that followed, Pilate had Roman soldiers dressed in peasant garb slip in among the protesters and had them attack the crowd at a prearranged signal; 3) a Samaritan prophet took a large crowd of people up to Mount Gerazim to show them holy vessels that he claimed Moses had hidden there. Pilate viewed this as an insurrection, and sent in the infantry and cavalry to attack the crowd, killing the prophet and many others. This last act caused him to be recalled to Rome.

* Only one significant mention of Pilate occurs in the gospels outside of the Passion narrative, and it has more in common with Josephus or Philo. Luke 13:1 refers to "Galileans whose blood Pilate had mingled with their sacrifices." The most likely scenario is that the Galileans were in Jerusalem for Passover, offering sacrifices at the temple. Passover, with its memories of liberation, was a time of heightened anxiety for the Roman authorities, and it would not have taken very much instigation for Pilate to react harshly.

* Although the gospels each give their own distinctive emphasis to Pilate, all of them present him as a conflicted figure. This likely has less to do with historical fact and more to do with a desire to show Roman authorities that Christians harbor no threat to them (since worshiping a criminal executed by the Romans was a problematic proposition to begin with). Mark has Pilate wonder at Jesus' silence (15:5) and asks the crowd what evil he has done (15:14). Matthew introduces Pilate's wife, who warns him to have nothing to do with "that righteous man" about whom she has had bad dreams (27:19). Matthew also has the famous scene of Pilate washing his hands, declaring his innocence of Jesus' blood, and the Jewish crowd's statement: "His blood be on us and on our children!" (27:24-25). In Luke, Pilate transfers Jesus to Herod Antipas because he is a Galilean (23:6-7). John's Pilate is the most reluctant to condemn Jesus (18:28—19:16), and asks Jesus the enigmatic question "What is truth?" (18:38).

All of the scriptural references to Pilate are contained in the following excerpt from the film *The Passion of the Christ* located at 41:00–44:00.

The film was extremely controversial because of its depiction of the Jews as the evil ones and not the Romans. Some scholars think that the gospels were written in this way to show Roman authorities that Christians harbored no threat to them and so that the writings had a better chance of escaping Roman censorship and destruction. It is clear from historical sources that Pilate was an extremely evil man.

But what about the Jews? Let's look also tonight at that part of Pilate's power structure in Jerusalem at the time. Who were these People of the Passion, the "people" in whom we are most called to see ourselves in the Passion narrative, the only "people" around? The majority were Pharisees, believers in following the letter of the law handed down from Moses and elaborated over centuries. Their very positions depended on the preservation of the law, so a threat to the validity of the law was as frightening to them as disorder in the streets was to the Roman authorities. Jesus threatened the status quo of both components of the structure of life in first-century Israel, a threat that they always met with destruction. Their commitment to their belief system was so rigid that they could not see or hear the good news of Jesus Christ. But there was one, Nicodemus, in whom my beloved husband Pettus most saw himself as he engaged in his last Lenten self-examination. I would like to share Pettus' favorite description of this individual, a slight paraphrase of the first sermon that our firstborn heard on the Sunday after her father's pancreatic cancer diagnosis, Lent 2002, and invite us to look for ourselves in him as Pettus did. Not only will we have a little more complete picture of the power structure in first-century Israel than just the Romans, but we can see that not all the "people" were deaf and blind to the message of Jesus Christ.

Nicodmus is identified by *The Interpreter's Dictionary of the Bible* not only as a "ruler of the Jews," not only as *a* teacher, but as *the* teacher. This pre-eminent Jewish official undoubtedly possessed great wealth, because he later provided approximately 75-100 pounds of myrrh and aloes "to be placed between the folds of the linen cloth in which the body of Jesus was wrapped for burial."[3]

In his message, "Nick and Joe Saved Easter," Pastor Andy Stanley says that Nicodemus' provision of the embalming materials and his participation with Joseph of Arimathea in embalming Jesus' body after the crucifixion proves beyond a shadow of a doubt that Jesus died. Even if Jesus had not died from crucifixion, he would have been dead after being wrapped, head and body, in over 100 pounds of spices and wet cloths. To the extent that Christianity hinges on a single event — that Jesus died and rose from the dead — Nicodemus' embalming of Jesus was proof in the first century of

Jesus' death.[4]

Who was this Nicodemus? Let us hear a slightly paraphrased lesson about Nicodemus from The Rev. Dr. Samuel T. Lloyd III at Trinity Church, Boston.

If Nicodemus had come to my church, he probably would have sat about three fourths of the way back, just over on the right. Some Sundays, he would have slipped in early to hear the choir rehearse and to have a few minutes of peace and quiet to let his racing mind throttle down at least a little. He would have loved the anonymity of this big place, the room to be left alone to wonder about God and his own life. And he probably would have slipped out quietly at the end, with nothing more than a nod to the priest at the door.

Nicodemus is our contemporary: looking for answers but playing it safe. He wants to find God, but he isn't at all sure what would happen if he did. He's looking for something more in his life but reluctant to take a risk.

"Now there was a Pharisee named Nicodemus, a leader of the Jews. He came to Jesus by night..." So John begins the story of this proud, cautious man who wants to meet this teacher from the hills of Galilee. The Pharisee is a powerful figure: a "leader of the Jews," maybe one of the Sanhedrin, the Supreme Court for the Jewish people.

Jesus is making quite a stir. Many see him as dangerous. But others say he knows God. He speaks with authority. And Nicodemus wants to see for himself, but privately, by night, when no one could spot him, no one would know of his meeting with this noisy outsider.

If it were not so profound, Nicodemus' conversation with Jesus would sound ludicrous. They keep talking, but there isn't much communication: "Rabbi, we know that you are a teacher who has come from God..." "We know," the words of an insider, maybe a little smug, a little pretentious. Let's talk, Jesus, teacher to teacher, Marine to Marine. We know what's up here. We know how God works and doesn't.

But Jesus' response sails right past that cozy beginning. "I'll tell you, no one can see the kingdom of God without being born from above."

Where did that come from? So much for a friendly little chat. We are not talking about a safe journey to know God just a little better. Jesus says, "You have to be born from above, or born again": the Greek word can mean either, or perhaps, both.

Born again: That's a phrase that has been so badly used by some to shut down thinking and exploration and growth. You won't need to question any more after you are born again.

But of course Jesus was opening up life's possibilities, not closing them down. You have to start over, he was saying, with a life and energy from beyond you. You want to have your same old life and God too. But it won't work that way.

"The terrible thing," C.S. Lewis wrote years ago, "the almost impossible thing, is to hand over your whole self: all your wishes and precautions, to Christ. But it is far easier than what we are all trying to do instead. For what we are trying to do is to remain 'ourselves,' to keep personal happiness our great aim, and yet at the same time to be 'good.' We are all trying to let our mind and heart go their own way: centered on money or pleasure or ambition, and hoping, in spite of this, to behave honestly and chastely and humbly. And that is exactly what Christ warned us you could not do."[5] You need to start over, Jesus said. Born again.

A Methodist minister named Howard Mumma was serving an American church in Paris in the 1950s when he noticed in the back of the church a man in a dark suit surrounded by admirers, and eventually the two met and developed a close friendship. The man was the great writer Albert Camus.

There had always been rumors that Camus was drawn

to Christian faith, but he had never converted. Mumma remembers him saying one evening, "The reason I have been coming to church is because I am seeking. I'm almost on a pilgrimage: seeking something to fill the void I am experiencing... I am searching for something the world is not giving me."

Camus knew the Bible well, and of all the characters there, the one he was most drawn to was Nicodemus. In talking about Nicodemus one day, Camus asked Mumma, "What does it mean to be born again, to be saved?" And Mumma replied, "To me to be born again is to enter anew or afresh into the process of spiritual growth. It is to receive forgiveness. It is to wipe the slate clean. You are ready to move ahead, to commit yourself to new life, a new spiritual pilgrimage."

Mumma reports that at that, Camus looked at him with tears in his eyes and said, "Howard, I am ready. I want this. This is what I want to commit my life to." Shortly after this conversation happened, Camus died in a car accident at age 46.[6]

Born again: It's an offer Camus found compelling. It sounds daunting, but it's an invitation and a promise that there's more and deeper life ahead.

Of course, Nicodemus has no idea what Jesus is talking about. "How can anyone be born after growing old? Can one enter a second time into the mother's womb and be born?"

But Jesus then confuses things even more: "No one can enter the kingdom of God without being born of water and Spirit. The wind blows; you hear the sound. You do not know where it comes from or where it is going." Water, wind, Spirit: those are the keys to this new life.

John the Baptist was baptizing in the Jordan River with water of washing, cleansing. Rebirth means naming where we've been caught, stuck in sin, confessing it, and starting again.

Rebirth happens in the Spirit, which is to say we do not

do it ourselves. It comes from beyond us, like the wind. You know what wind is. It is the air that is around you all the time, like God's presence. You don't notice it because it is in everything. But sometimes the air starts moving. You can't tell where it comes from, or where it's going. Rebirth is like that. God moving, stirring.

Being born again may bring with it God's summons to give our time or our money to a cause that matters. It may mean a decision actually to plunge into classes and let this Christian faith take you to a new place. It may mean asking why we were put on earth: What is the gift only you or I can give to the world?

And one thing is clear: This new birth isn't planned. It isn't something you can set out to do. It is, to use our gospel's term, "from above." Something happens to you and gets hold of you when you're not looking.

Well, poor Nicodemus still doesn't get it and says, "How can this be?" And at that Jesus takes him to the heart of the matter: God so loved the world, that he gave his only Son, so that everyone who believes in him may not [be lost] but may have eternal life. Martin Luther called this the gospel in summary.

I can't give you four easy steps to a new life, Jesus is saying. God is doing something so much grander than that. The Creator of the universe loves you, yes you, enough to hang on a cross to set you free from the sting of sin and death. The answer to your search is to accept that love and to let yourself be led by the Spirit's breeze.

We aren't told what happened to Nicodemus as a result of his nighttime meeting. Apparently nothing did immediately. It must have taken some time for it all to sink in. But something shifted somewhere, because we see him two more times. He's in the temple later when Jesus is being accused by crowds demanding he be arrested. One man stands up to defend him. His name is Nicodemus.

And at the very end, Jesus is dead, crucified, and there is Nicodemus. This time he isn't there at night as a seeker, but as a disciple, helping take Jesus' body away.

The man who came with his questions, who couldn't make heads or tails of it all, somehow GETS IT by the end. Nicodemus said "yes" to God. He followed Christ. He was born anew. It made all the difference.

And it can for us too.[7]

Let's take a moment to examine these questions.

---

1. *Book of Common Prayer*, p. 832.

2. *Book of Common Prayer*, p. 264.

3. George A. Buttrick, *The Interpreter's Dictionary of the Bible*, Vol. 3 (Nashville, Tennessee: Abingdon Press, 1962), p. 547.

4. http://www.sermoncentral.com/sermons/nick-and-joe-save-easter-andy-stanley-sermon-on-easter-resurrection-176057.asp?Page=13.

5. C.S. Lewis, *Mere Christianity* (New York: Macmillan Publishing Company, 1952), p. 168.

6. Howard Mumma, *Albert Camus and the Minister* (Brewster, Massachusetts: Paraclete Press, 2000).

7. The Rev. Dr. Samuel T. Lloyd III, "The Night Visitor," sermon at Trinity Episcopal Church, February 22, 2002.

QUESTIONS
(for small group discussion or journaling)

What about yourself did you see in Pilate? In Nicodemus?

What do you wish you had seen?

What do you wish you had NOT seen and need to let go?

Then let us go in silence as we depart this place and open our hands to let go of the stones at the foot of the Cross.

Week Five
Judas

Let us pray
Almighty and eternal God, so draw our hearts to you, so guide our minds, so fill our imaginations, so control our wills, that we may be wholly yours, utterly dedicated to you; and then use us, we pray, as you will, and always to your glory and the welfare of your people; through our Lord and Savior Jesus Christ. Amen.

Joan Chittister writes in her work *The Rule of Benedict* that "growth is not an accident. Growth is a process. We have to want to grow. We have to work at uprooting the weeds that are smothering good growth in ourselves. We have to will to move away the stones that entomb us in ourselves."[1] My most fervent prayer is that this journey with the People of the Passion is helping you in moving away the stones that entomb you in yourself, as it is doing for me.

In observance of a Holy Lent, we have remembered together the People of the Passion, looked for ourselves in them, and allowed the growth for which we were created. Tonight we are also called to forget. In talking about the epistle where Paul speaks of "forgetting what lies behind... I press on toward the goal... the upward call of God in Christ Jesus," the March 25, 2007, *Forward Day by Day* says, "My desks both at home and at school groan under the weight of old papers and books. My shoulders often ache from carrying old griefs and guilt. My heart is heavy with unresolved sorrows. All this is what Paul would have me lay down, forget, 'count as refuse,' in order to respond with grace and agility to that upward call. 'Forgetting' this part of my past would free me to turn to our Lord, with gladness and singleness of heart."[2]

[Let us be reminded once again of our purpose here: the purpose of this Lenten weekly study on the People of the Passion is the very purpose of Lent as defined in the *Book of Common Prayer*:

> *To observe with great devotion the days of Jesus' suffering and resurrection.*
> *It is the Church's custom to prepare for this observance by "a season of penitence and fasting... (because) of the need which all Christians continually have to renew repentance and faith...*
> *(The Church invites us) to the observance of a Holy Lent by self-examination and repentance; by prayer, fasting, and self-denial; and by reading and meditating on God's holy word."*[3]

As we go through that "self-examination," I invite you once again to hold in your hand a piece of stone. Its edges are sharp and jagged as if broken. We have a choice this week — and every week of Lent — as to what to do with those stones. We can hang onto them as painful reminders of our separation from God, making us broken people. Or we can let them go; we can lay them at the foot of the Cross and open our hands and hearts so that we can move closer to God and God can fill us with love and forgiveness, healing, and grace.

So as we examine these People of the Passion, let us look for us in them, for those characteristics that we need to lay at the foot of the Cross during this Lent. And perhaps on this Easter morning the stone will be moved away for us, just as it was on that first Easter morning.]

Our recurring motif of nearness vs. separation, blessed vs. sinful, has threaded through the study of these People of the Passion, these individuals who were witnesses of Christ's Passion. The extent to which these individuals stayed close to Christ is the extent to which they were blessed and became Easter people. Mary, mother of Jesus, and Mary Magdalene stayed close, and they saw the resurrection. Peter crossed and recrossed and recrossed the threshold of hope from separation to nearness, just as we do, but once he perceived the hope of the resurrection, he got it too and spent the rest of his life staying near to his risen Lord. Nicodemus too gradually crossed the threshold from opponent to disciple.

Pontius Pilate, on the other hand, chose to separate from Jesus.

By studying Nicodemus at the same time as Pilate, we saw that they both were men full of questions. Pilate asked: "Are you the King of the Jews?" and "What is truth?" While Nicodemus asked: "How can one be born from above?"

The responses of these two questioners could not have been more different: at the Passion of our Lord, when the other Pharisees were shouting "Crucify him! Crucify him!" Nicodemus stayed close, helping to take him down from the Cross and bury him. Pilate separated, sending him to his death. Both had free will, just as we do, but they exercised it differently. This devotional says, "We need not collude in Christ's crucifixion, as the religious authorities of Jesus' day did, or stand by and watch it happen, as Pilate did. We have choices about who we will be in this drama, and the choices are ours alone. If we do not actively choose the good, we are very likely passively to choose evil."[4]

We can see the effects of staying close to Jesus vs. separating from him as we look at all the People of the Passion we are studying this Lent.

NEAR ——————————————————————— FAR
Mary Mary Magdalene Peter Pilate Nicodemus   Judas

LET'S LOOK THIS WEEK AT JUDAS:

* According to Brent Landau, Judas was one of the twelve disciples of Jesus known for providing Jesus' enemies with his whereabouts so that they can arrest him.

* The name "Judas" is common enough (several other Judases are mentioned in the New Testament), but the surname "Iscariot" is a mystery. Two main theories exist, neither without problems. One, first advanced by the ancient Christian commentator Jerome, thinks it is a transliteration of the Hebrew *Ish-Kerioth*, "man of Kerioth," a collection of small towns in Judea. This would mark Judas as distinct from the other disciples, who all hail from Galilee, but if this is its meaning, it was obliterated by the time the gospels were written. The other suggestion is that it is a corruption of the Greek *sikarios*, a term for a kind of Jewish assassin, but it is unclear whether the *sikarioi* existed during Jesus' ministry.

* Judas receives more attention as the gospel tradition develops. In Mark's gospel (the earliest), he only appears by name in the list of the twelve disciples (3:19), in his visit to the chief priests to arrange the betrayal (14:10), and his kiss of identification in the garden (14:43-45). But Jesus also states that it would be better if the one who betrayed the Son of Man was never born (14:21).

Luke provides a few more details: Satan has entered Judas (22:3); Judas attempts to kiss Jesus, but Jesus says: "Judas, is it with a kiss that you are betraying the Son of Man?" (22:48).

Matthew's details: Judas requests money for the betrayal (26:15); Judas "plays dumb" at the Last Supper (26:25); at seeing Jesus condemned to death, Judas tries to return the money, and failing, he commits suicide (27:3-5).

John's details: Judas criticizes a woman who anoints Jesus' feet for the waste of money, despite stealing from the common purse in his role as the group treasurer (12:4-6); Jesus gives Judas a piece of bread at the Last Supper to signify his betrayal, Satan enters him, and he goes out into the night (13:26-30).

* The manner in which Judas dies becomes a point of interest for several early Christian texts. In Matthew 27:5-8, he commits suicide by hanging himself, and the priests use his returned blood money to buy a field, called the "Field of Blood," in which to bury foreigners. In Acts 1:17-18, Judas buys a field with his reward money and then bursts open in his mid-section and his bowels spill out; because of this, the field becomes known as the "Field of Blood." In traditions known to Papias of Hieropolis, a Christian bishop of the early second century, Judas swelled up to such a degree that he could not pass through a space the width of a wagon; parts of his body became enlarged to grotesque proportions; he died on his own land, which smelled so foul that it was never inhabited again.

* In 2006, the National Geographic Society financed the purchase and publication of a fragmentary manuscript containing a work called the *Gospel of Judas*. The existence of this document was only previously known through a few citations by early church writers, who state that it makes Judas out to be a hero who does Jesus' bidding in the betrayal. The *Gospel of Judas* dates from the second century, and few scholars believe that it records any reliable historical data.

* The name "Judas" has become so synonymous with betrayal that virtually no Christians name their sons this. At one point, it was illegal in Germany to even name one's dog Judas.

Let's look at a depiction of Judas' betrayal and one of his suicide in this excerpt from the film *The Passion of the Christ* located at 32:00–33:55 and 35:35–38:10.

Mary, Mary Magdalene, Peter, and Nicodemus opened their hands and their hearts to Jesus. They remembered him always, staying close, forgetting themselves, and thereby remembering themselves. Pilate and Judas were dismembered by choosing to separate from him.

But as different as the responses of these People of the Passion and as ours are, there is one thing that is identical in every case. The answer is in Romans 8:38-39: "Neither death nor life, neither angels nor demons, neither the present nor the future, nor any powers, neither height nor depth, nor anything else in all creation, will be able to separate us from the love of God that is in Christ Jesus our Lord."

As we conclude tonight, let's look again at that excerpt from *The Passion of the Christ* depicting Mary Magdalene as she reaches up to Jesus after her first encounter with him and of her accusers dropping their stones, located at 1:06:11–1:07:45. Nothing she did and nothing we do can ever separate us from his love. Opening our hands and our hearts as we reach up to him will keep us close and keep us blessed all the days of our lives.

Let's take a moment to examine these questions.

---

1. Joan Chittister, *The Rule of Benedict: Insights for the Ages* (New York: Crossroad Publishing Company, 1992), p. 120.

2. Anonymous, *Forward Day by Day* (Cincinnati, Ohio: Forward Movement, February 21, 2007).

3. *Book of Common Prayer*, p. 264.

4. Browning, March 26.

QUESTIONS
(for small group discussion or journaling)

What about yourself did you see in Judas?

What do you wish you had seen?

What do you wish you had NOT seen and need to let go?

Then let's walk in silence as we depart this place and open our hands to let go of the stones at the foot of the Cross.

For Further Reading

Ann Brock, *Mary Magdalene, the First Apostle: The Struggle for Authority* (Cambridge, MA: Harvard University Press, 2003)

Raymond E. Brown, Joseph A. Fitzmyer, Karl P. Donfried, *Mary in the New Testament* (Mahwah, NJ: Paulist Press, 1978)

Bart Ehrman, *Peter, Paul, and Mary Magdalene: The Followers of Jesus in History and Legend* (Oxford, UK: Oxford University Press, 2006)

Steven Hijmans, "In Search of St. Peter's Tomb," http://www.uofaweb.ualberta.ca/classics/news.cfm?story=27355

His Holiness Pope John Paul II, *Crossing the Threshold of Hope* (New York: Knopf, 1995)

Karen King, *The Gospel of Mary of Magdala: Jesus and the First Woman Apostle* (Salem, OR: Polebridge Press, 2003)

Steven Molin, *Journey of Stones: A Sermon Series for Lent and Easter* (Lima, OH: CSS Publishing Company, 2003)

Jaroslav Pelikan, David Flusser, Justin Lang, *Mary: Images of the Mother of Jesus in Jewish and Christian Perspective* (Minneapolis, MN: Fortress Press, 2005)

Jane Schaberg, *The Illegitimacy of Jesus* (Sheffield, UK: Sheffield Academic Press, 1990)

CPSIA information can be obtained
at www.ICGtesting.com
Printed in the USA
FSHW022354210220
67194FS